From the Center

From the Center

Poetic Prayers and Meditations

Robert J. Hope

Foreword by

William A. Meninger, o.c.s.o.

Continuum
New York • London

2001

The Continuum International Publishing Group Inc
370 Lexington Avenue, New York, NY 10017

The Continuum International Publishing Group Ltd
The Tower Building, 11 York Road, London SE1 7NX

Printed in the United States of America

Library of Congress Cataloging-in-Publication Data

Hope, Robert J.
From the center : poetic prayers and meditations ; foreword by
Wiliam A. Meninger / Robert J. Hope.
p. cm.
ISBN 0-8264-1324-2 (alk. paper)
1. Meditations.   2. Prayers.   I. Title.

BV4832.3 .H67 2001
242—dc21   00-052345

Contents

Contents

Contents

Contents

Foreword

Bob Hope is a mystic. That's no big deal, so am I—and probably most of the people who will read and reflect on this book. The days are long past when mystics were seen to be consumptive nuns languishing in the throes of Teresian swoons, with occasional Lenten stigmata. Today they are more apt to be businessmen, retirees like Bob (with a basketball in the backseat of the car, "just in case"), secretaries, teachers, policemen, and even priests and nuns!

Evelyn Underhill defines a mystic as one who seeks union with God without the use of intermediaries. This is why those who have the charism of providing intermediaries often hold mystics suspect and why mystics are usually driven to express their experiences in poetry rather than in theology. Where there is no intermediary, there is no speculation (theologizing)—only union (love). To pass judgment on a mystic, one must be a mystic, a poet, and a theologian. This is why I think that *From the Center* would meet the approval of an Augustine, a Bernard, or a Teresa.

The Cloud of Unknowing, a fourteenth-century treatise on contemplative prayer and the source of the Centering Prayer, which qualifies Bob as a mystic, expresses this beautifully: "[S/he] whom the mind cannot grasp, the heart can embrace." Or, to put it more prosaically, we can never really know God with our puny intellects (theology), but we definitely can hug God (love).

The author beautifully expresses this in his very first offering:

> *O, Blessed One, take me deep, deeper still,*
> *Where thought or image dare not go,*
> *But only a selfless I, and that soon lost*
> *In the silence of your You,*
> *Where we are one, where I am You.*

As a nod in the direction of ecumenism, it is worth noting here that in the Christian context love is the equivalent of nonduality in the Eastern religions. A poet (mystic) has no problem saying "Where we are one, where I am You." A theologian would have to inundate the page with footnotes.

Another marvelous statement from *The Cloud* finds frequent expression here in the intensity of poetic feeling. "We were made to love and everything else was made to make love possible." The author's "everything else" invites him to embrace a riot of colorful images from the erotic (not unexpectedly) to animals (especially birds) to the mundane (the Atlantic Ocean in his front yard). The contemplative attitude is found in all of us, especially in mystics, lovers, and children. It is both the prelude to and the result of contemplative meditation. It involves a sense of wonder at the universal presence of God and a personal experience of one's nothingness inextricably interwoven with the infinity of God's being (*Isness*). "There is life to be lived in the singularities of Nows given. All is gift—and I the gifted."

Genuine contemplation does not permit navel gazing. There are movements within and without. This motion is beautifully expressed as God "spilling goodness into the finite." At the same time, the paradox of every God-human relationship is always present:

> *Physics is not knowable.*
> *Magnitude mounts to mystery:*
> *How far the star that's farthest,*
> *How small the speck that's smallest?*
> ....
> *What is the realm of the real, Beloved:*
> *Only You, only You.*

To be in touch with God is to experience God in all the ways God truly is, to be quiet in the Center of one's being yet never still, in union of being but also in union of creation:

My soul is hungry.
It needs the feeding of your forces—
Water and wind,
Sky and song of bird,
The colors that make the world a joy,
....
Majestic One, let me come to the table
Of your world when I am hungry.

Perhaps with this lovely book, meditation according to *The Cloud of Unknowing* (Centering Prayer) has once again come of age. There are thousands of people who will welcome it with appreciation and understanding. I do not think this would have been true twenty-five years ago. Let this book speak to your heart as it does to mine.

WILLIAM A. MENINGER O.C.S.O.

Preface

God is Self-giving Unconditional Love loving us. Most of us know God loves us—from our childhood, when our parents told us; from homilies throughout our lives; or, for some of us, from our theological studies. But knowing conceptually, theologically, that God loves us is like eating the menu and not the meal— what our Buddhist brethren tell us "points to the moon but is not the moon." It seems to me that each one's spiritual journey is simply getting more and more in touch with that already is: the infinite God loving us unconditionally every moment of our existence. For me this happens most in the vacuity of that apophatic mode called Centering Prayer.

There is no task that is prerequisite to God's love—our true selves are already loved. In fact, it is the *growing* experience of this love that empowers us to shed the enslaving and deadening demands of our false selves. We give up the self we are not to be the self that we already are—a unique beloved of God.

So true, so satisfying, is the fullness of that experienced relationship that it subsumes all human values, all joys, all pain, all teaching, and spawns every act of requiting love. The dynamic power of God's passionate, unconditional, constant, transforming love draws us ever deeper into life itself—until at last we discover who we are, our true identity, *a beloved of God.* Left behind are all the pretenses that bind us to death. Like Pharaoh's army, they die in the silent sea of God's love. Beneath the self that dies is the self that lives. How can we continue to condemn ourselves if God so loves us! Or how continue to feel unworthy if God's love makes us lovable. A wholeness happens, an integrity in our responding love wherein everything is known with that holistic knowledge born of love. Nothing thereafter can be ugly, no core unclean, for love transforms us. Epiphanies appear in every *now* to one who knows that one is beloved. The numinous is in the Eden of the everyday. A star, a stone, a single flower shouts hosannas. And life is lived to the fullest.

Thomas Merton sagaciously points out that the journey to the true self and the journey to God are one and the same journey. It is only in relationship with God that we find our true selves. For me this ever deepening relationship is best occasioned and realized in the kenotic silence of Centering Prayer. Centering Prayer is a form of apophatic prayer in which we let go of all thought and simply consent to the presence and action of God within.

Like most, my continuing journey into that relationship had a significant happening. It was on the day in the mid-seventies when I went with a group to St. Joseph's Abbey in Spencer, Massachusetts. Abbot Thomas Keating taught us Centering Prayer, and guest master and former classmate of mine Trappist William Meninger gave me his Centering Prayer tapes. My daily practice of Centering Prayer began then and has continued, augmented later by the daily practice of *Lectio Divina* and journaling. Over the years the prose of my journaling found more poetic expression. This book comprises a selection from that journaling. I never know what I'm going to write each day and rarely remember what I've just written. I write not from my head but from my Center—whether it be after Centering Prayer, *Lectio*, or a numinous experience in nature. Simply put, it is grateful, responsive prayer to the Self-giving God of unconditional love.

How grateful, then, I am to Thomas Keating for the gift of Centering Prayer and for his teachings, which I have come to know well as a commissioned presenter of Centering Prayer and a New England coordinator for Contemplative Outreach, the organization that Thomas Keating founded and still indefatigably heads. But mostly I am grateful for his authentic witness to what it means to be a beloved.

He is both beacon and path for me in my continuing journey.

I am grateful, too, to William Meninger for his friendship and guidance when we sometimes join in presenting Centering Prayer. And to Basil Pennington, who with Thomas and William began the Centering Prayer movement, which has grown so and has borne such evident fruit in more contemplative living by both lay people and clergy of different religious persuasions.

Vincent McKiernan, Paulist priest and friend, first encouraged me to publish. (I admit to vexing ambivalence; it felt like sharing intimate personal letters with the world. But I doubt God, who calls us to oneness, is offended by expressions of deep sharing.) Thank you, Vinny.

And I am grateful to the staff and community at the Paulist Center in Boston, where I have worshiped, served, and been served for over thirty years.

As a recipient of the periodical *Friends of Silence,* founded and edited by Nan C. Merrill, I came to know her. Nan has read the manuscript and made helpful suggestions. I am very grateful to her for her insights.

I am grateful also to those who meet with me each week to pray *Lectio* and Centering Prayer, which so supports my own daily prayer. And to the many groups over the past twenty-five years with whom I prayed weekly. And lastly to all those people who came to my Centering Prayer workshops, for their acceptance, enthusiasm, insights, and discernible love.

I thank my wife, Sylvia, for handling all the processing preparations and details at which I am so inept. I am grateful for my children, Monica and Rachel, just because they are so lovely.

Mostly I am grateful to the God of unconditional love who calls me to the richness of Presence at the center of myself—out of which flow words that never say but only point.

Finally, it is my hope that *From the Center* will occasion in the reader an ever deepening union with the God who is Unconditional Love.

R. J. H.

O, Blessed One, take me deep, deeper still,
Where thought or image dare not go,
But only a selfless I, and that soon lost
In the silence of your You,
Where we are one, where I am You.

Beloved, keep me ever open.
Let nothing distract,
No care concern,
No pleasure pull,
Nothing rich rob.
Let my lamp be lit,
Oil aplenty.
Always receiving the Bridegroom,
That I be in the banquet
Where world goods are given gladly,
Exchanged for the God-good.
God emptying into guest
And guest into God
And the feast begin
And chamber prepared
For eternal love.

O Great Mystery, how deep is deep?
Infinite the plummeting,
For You are infinite.
There is no end then to my fall.
Down, down in delight I descend.
Bottomless the plunge,
Always farther down.
Called to union by love of Lover,
Free from surface struggles.
Only calm and thoughtless silence
Giving rise to joy.
Deep, deep You call me.
Union within union
Till one there only be.
Call me, Love,
Down, down from surface,
That I forever plummet.

I must go to the You who *is,*
Deep in the Center of all
Where the real begins
And all being is born.
There am I born in every Now,
Deep, deep, deep in the Center
That is the Center, the One of the many,
Wholly immanent, wholly transcendent.
There must I go—to the mystery of *is*—
And offer praise and sacrifice.

Life of my life, let dry this pen.
Make void my mind,
No word escape.
Let darkness blind my eyes,
Silence my ears,
No sense seek satisfaction,
Denied if it does.
Then let me know your presence
In the dark and silence of my soul
And in that place of silence
Know your love.
And all riddance be then joy
For in their going I be filled,
In their absence your love
And my love begotten.
Ah my soul's source,
My Lover and my God,
Take me ever deeper,
That in the knowing I stretch
Vulnerably to infinity.

Oh to be emptied out of self.
And from my core write letters to my God.
Letters without words, saying without
    symbol.
Love alone be plenteous statement,
Nothing fractured in utterance,
No self-seeking sought.
Love and only love,
A never ending love,
Poured out to my never ending God.
Love begot from love.
What is received, given back
In infinite exchange.
God's resplendent love
Sourcing my own.
And I have not to do with words again.
Thou, make me empty.
Slay what You must.

I am hungry, Creator,
My soul is hungry.
It needs the feeding of your forces—
Water and wind,
Sky and song of bird,
The colors that make the world a joy,
And the kiss of elements
With each other.
See, the gull glides,
Sitting on unseen air.
The water waves in shades of blue,
Prodded by wind to meet the shore.
The sailboat in silent rhythm
Sails with wind and wave
To blanch a sail against the blue.
And a rise of rocks
On a distant shore
Carves shape beyond expanse.
These are the food and force
That feed my soul.
Majestic One, let me come to the table
Of your world when I am hungry.

Where went the when that was?
Wafting forever out,
Woven into eternal Now,
Never lost.
Always an is that is,
Though a when that was.
No sequence in the heart of God,
Only a Now that holds the numinous
Of each of the whens that were
But are in God's eternal Now.

Divine Lover, take me ever deeper.
There in the core of the self
Will I know who I am.
Where no one's name may reach,
Nor will I call myself a name.
There in the Center I shall be lost,
With no need for name.
The knowing will be a knowing of You.
And You have no name—
Nor then will I.
O Beloved of my heart,
Take me so deep that I am lost—
A great losing that finds
And finds forever.

Holy my Center and deep as infinity,
The hallowed place I go to *be.*
From there all that's me becomes
And all my essence flows.
Holy, holy, holy,
This place where You reside,
Deep within, the infinite One,
Infinitely available if I but go.
Calling as lover to beloved.
An eternal embrace
That makes me one
With the Maker of my being
Till I am no longer I,
But Love made manifest.
Holy, holy, holy, the Core of my core.

Beloved, let me look at loveliness this day.
For You are loveliness,
And if a flower fades,
Let me consent
And find You in another form.
From form to form You leap—
Restless to render the world anew.
And if I stay behind to mourn,
I shall miss the latest loveliness
And the beauty of your face.
So let me look at loveliness
All this whole day long.

Merciful One, loose my tongue stilled in
    silence.
Let it speak to this world's woes
And, rich from silence, waken hope,
Illumined in the dark therein.
Let word wade into
A world too long weary.
Let it break bonds and feed hunger
And slake the waterless.
Let it form flesh on bones too naked
And announce a Love that heals.
This would I take from silence.
But let first the silence thicken
And the dark be marriage chamber
Where union charge me
With your wordless Word.

Where is the winter?
There is none in my Center,
The place of your Presence,
The fullness and the filled.
So let ice form and snow fly,
Let creep cold with freezing claws,
Let niveous night bespeak the cold.
You are in my Center,
Where no ice or frost can come.
Only You, with eternal love
And infinite in your Presence.
Blessed One, take me to my Center,
Where winter never comes.

Another day to move me
On the surface of your real,
Where things abound
And acts uncountable happen,
Where flowers give glory, and birds, joy,
And all the creatures of the world
Are in the throes of time.
Yet there is a Center to it all—
A Center that is still
And source of all the real.
No real is real without it be.
It is a Now real—
No time dare pass nor act happen.
Yet all the peace and joy and all that is
Flares forth from this still and really real
At the Center, the deepest part of me.
For at the center of my Center is You.

Such primal sonancy,
All is Eden in my hearing:
The concert of rhythmic patters
Rain upon mixed textures;
Birds bent on expression
Sow sound sweetly, softly,
Dimly from a distance.
From out the fog
A horn moans its primordial om
In resonance with the primal erg
That spins the world to wonderment.
All is Eden for the hearing,
Yes, and in any given Now.
You are everywhere for the listening.
Glory, glory to the God who sings!

The land lies lovely under Love's sky.
Flowers stretch to kiss the sun,
Birds in aerial ballet—
Color, shape, and motion
Weave a one.
Yes, the many as a one.
And I have a place in the one
So let me take my place,
Amid marvels that stretch to stars.
For how can I be part of the one
If I stay only an only.
Beloved, put me in my place.

I write what's not written,
For writing writes the finite.
And the finite is never finished,
Forever finding more.
Only when words wane
Do I again seek source
Till I find the infinite
That fuels the never ending finite.
O Author of the all,
I've filled of finite.
Let me let it go
And plummet to the infinite
In a free fall to Center,
Where in stillness and in silence
You source a world of words.

The power of the present pulls me in,
Ever gripping, grabbing, drawing.
There is a world within a world,
And You are there,
Sourcing all from nothingness—
Stillness, only stillness in the movement,
Quiet, only quiet in the sound,
The eternal Now,
Not bounded by movement of the many,
And in its freedom, so am I.
Blessed One, it is good for me to be here.
Shall I make a tent?

Source of all, You render reality rich.
No mind can fathom
Inexhaustible treasures
Thrown from stars
Spewing the riches of reality,
Blasting vacuity into fullness.
Energy everywhere,
Marrying and marrying.
And now I stand beneath the stars
That made me,
Beneath the cliffs that bore me,
Under the clouds that rained me.
Eternal One, let me marry my elements,
Those I meet in my Nows,
And may our offspring, too, give glory
In your never ending Now.

Kiss me, Beloved,
That I may kiss You back.
Let sun and sea and sky
Be lips that kiss,
And I whelmed by the witness of their kiss,
Drawn to offer my own parched lips
In witness of requiting love.
Let me tryst with You, Love—
The place be anywhere
In the everywhere.
It is I who need to go—
And find the place
Where You would kiss
And, in that gentle way,
Love me—
And I to love you back.
Beloved, when I see the wonders of the
    world,
Let them be for me your lips,
Pressing tenderly to mine—
And so to kiss
And give self forgettingly away.

Being and form come tumbling into time
And there in their midst am I.
Being with form, form with being,
The world is soaked with being.
Forms ramble in the range of the real
'Til, tumbling, skipping, twisting,
Twirling, tilting this way, that,
Forms form, fade, and form again,
Pushed by being, pulsing with existence.
Such is the world to which I wake—
A form with being—
Pulsing with existence before I fade
And flesh form another form
While You and I are one.

Beloved, who am I that You should love me
    so!
A leaf asked to let go
And sail to place upon a pond
Where wind and rain play a bit
Before I sink to the drawing depths
And know You as You are.

And so I ask and gently plead,
And You, Creator, grant.
I ask for the Spirit,
That I be filled with fullness,
The goodness in every Now,
Waking to the wonder of your Presence,
With heart lost to none but You
As You give yourself to me.
Oh Holy One,
Maker of all that is, and me,
Immerse me in the real,
The holy home of your Presence.
I've too long lain in illusion,
Lost and eating pods of pigs.
Forgiver of the lost, send the Spirit,
And take me home to You.
The child of your making asks You.

Smote are the powers that plague.
On every side the philistine falls,
For the Heart of all hearts is in my Center
And my right arm is raised by Love.
Though the solace of my Center is peace,
Peace in You is strength—
Strength no warrior can withstand.
Its sword is truth,
And the stone it hurls, love.
And all foes fall from its force.
It is You who give victory
To the David in me,
Who slays all my false-self foes.

Take me to my Center.
I ache for the Ark of your Presence,
You in my holy of holies,
All that could ever be written in stone,
The all of everything.
No truth truthful but it come from You,
No good, good, no beauty, beautiful.
You are the *isness* of the each
And the unity of the all.
And You are housed
In the temple of my Center.
Who am I, Divine Guest,
That You should be so one with me?

Beloved, I sit here in your weather.
The stand of strands mat,
Pushed rudely by your wind.
A cormorant struggling somewhere,
And rain drums stuttering on my roof.
But all is one, all is one
On this verdant margin of the lake—
The sky, the wind, the water,
And now the glide of gulls.
No thing complains and says,
"I'll not be part of this."
Each is in communion with the all,
Giving and taking in accord with need.
And think of that single blade of grass
Dancing with a forest of friends
Around this small lake
'Neath this rain-soaked sky
On this tiny earth
Orbiting in a world wonder-large.
And I, O Great Mystery, a pleased part of
    all.
Glory, glory to the God who *is!*

O Beloved, to be your butterfly,
Flitting where You will,
Trusting air and wind.
Color-called to riches,
Blue and red and yellow.
A resonance thralled by each
To linger in their loveliness
Before I flit to other.
There is life to be lived
In the singularities of Nows given.
All is gift—and I the gifted.

All things speak to me.
Now this color, now that shape,
Now the clear call of the loon.
The forest sees me coming
And each tree says, "Look at me.
See, I reveal the Beautiful."
A telling without words,
A bonding that breaks barriers of duality.
For is not the stuff of tree the stuff of me?
Do we not house the same Source?
Our union is one in God.
Unity is the one made of the many
By the inhering God.
We are one then, each a sibling.
So look at me—I give myself to you
And reveal the Beautiful One.

A single sparrow—
You know when it falls.
And know, though plentiful,
The hairs of my head,
The myriad *isnesses* that are one.
And You know each so well.
What fish swims no longer
Yet is ever in your mind?
What spider with patience coiled
Strikes the hapless ant
Now, now this instant!
And how many spiders, how many ants!
If all do your bidding, Beloved,
Within their own,
Then let me in my doing
Be ever true to yours.
For am I not worth many sparrows?

Merciful Beloved, save me.
I am in a mirrored room.
When I contort to see You,
It is my false face I see.
Every face mine,
For You have no face.
Shatter what I cannot break, Love.
Let me escape this funhouse false
And fly to empty, silent Center
Where You are fully, faceless, present.
And more!—
Where I am fully present
In the silence and the dark
And in the full forgetting
Of all I ever knew.

There'll be a going forth
If there's a going in,
For the Center holds the world
In the One who made it.
And out of the love at the Center,
I am charged to go forth
To bring your love to the world.
For the power of your Presence
Is the strength of my doing.
Holy Energizer, take me deep
And charge me.

Foxes have dens, birds nests.
My resting place is You, Love,
You, the hollow where I rest.
Care shed like discarded clothes,
I rest vulnerably invulnerable,
In silent self-surrender,
Content, safe, and loved.
O fox, you furrow and find your hole.
O bird, you weave your wicker nest.
And I just sit,
Seated in my Center,
For there do I find rest.

Oh to know your love, Love,
That my own might crawl like a criminal
Beyond the guards of vanity,
Past the gates of illusion,
Out of a self that isn't
Into the self that is,
Out to boundless infinity,
Free to be who I am—
A beloved held in your Heart.

Newness, Great Creator!
Newness always unfolding.
New expressions, epiphanies.
Each flowering a form
Filled with the *isness* of your doing.
Being born, birthed in newness.
An always coming,
Myriad upon myriad, uncountable.
Each with a fresh filling of your face
For us to see and to be.
All from the primordial erg and om.
O Beloved Birther, You are eternally new,
Yet immutably same.
I, too, I shall ripple out your newness
To a world that is never the same.

Unholy the hour lost to vanity.
With no root in the real,
It sucks away the bliss of being
And never finds friends
In a world of them.

They are not long,
These days to be,
But a taste of eternity.
Yet in each day,
In each hour,
There is the power
Of a Now
That stretches timeless
In its core
And knows eternity
Be not more.

What is the doing to be done
Before the doing stops?
For the world is won by doing,
And I have so little left.
There is a niche notched for everything—
But whatever niche is notched
The world winds glorious new,
And even buried bones bleed purpose.

Where do squirrels hop—except into Nows?
No twitch without expectation, they,
No Now without the joy of living.
Though they scurry over bones
In yard of graves,
Death is far from mind.
They live in a Now and ask not.
They live in the bounty of your giving
And dance to the music of the cosmos,
Happy to be—in the dance of being.
Such is the trust of a squirrel.
Why not mine, Eternal Dancer, why not
    mine?

With hoary beard
The traceless sea
Pounds upon a stubborn shore.
Not gently does it sunder,
But with fury
Comes to thunderous end
And finds in the froth of its demise
Single droplet kin
So long journeying as one.
And if the sea,
I as well—
One with a world
I thought apart.
For Great Ocean of Love,
We are all, all
One in You.

Eons are but seconds
In the nows of your Now.
Mountains move like stallions
Gamboling over a land.
Life leaks from ocean floor,
Starting a journey to You.
How it darts this way and that,
Moving from whence it came,
In search of where to go.
And in the search, new life forms
And strives for fullness.
Life unlimited.
Out of the sea,
On land life crawls
To sire a fuller fullness in new forms.
And now, we've come, so very late,
And see where we have been,
Knowing the Source of our coming
Is the eternal Term of our going.

How long, O my Destiny,
Have these waters sparkled in the sun.
I will soon be gone,
My flesh to find another form.
But days filled with future suns
Will flash with festooned splendor
These willing waters roiled in wrinkles
Wedded to the wind.
Long, long, long after I am gone,
The three will shout their silent praise—
Sun and wind and water—
And another sit beside this lake
And witness with wonder and with praise,
While I in other form do same.

How old is old—young, young?
Being has no age;
So if my form be old,
My being is ever young . . .
Sliding into eternity
On the backs of Nows,
Never aging, always young.
This will I say a millenium from now.
Who knows what bones will wear
The flesh I've left?
Source of all being,
I am forever young in You.

Where do the dying die?
In the deserts of nowhere,
Where no one may come but they,
Deep in some forsaken place, the dying go
Alone to meet their Maker,
Leaving behind the all of their lives.
Even the loved ones are left,
Though hardest,
In the journey not of their making.
They go to die in the desert
Alone—utterly alone.
As they came to birth,
So they go to death—alone!
And, in that final letting go,
Come to You.
And it does not matter anymore
Whether barn and silo are filled.
They come to You!

Let me pull on the ropes of infinity
And clutch the hours of eternity,
Pulling them into my heart.
With uplifted arms
Will I encircle the All
And draw it to my bosom,
There to store You,
Held captive by your love for me.
For how can You let go your beloved?
How depart your place of Presence?
Neither will You wither away.
Always will You love me
In my inmost center.
Smaller than a measurement,
As large as infinity,
There in that deep place
Shall we be one:
The Maker and the made,
The Lover and the loved,
My Beloved and me as one.

And now the dimming time,
When light leaks less its brilliance
And all the loveliness of young
Calls less to sense.
Their world now, the young,
Theirs the meadow on which to skip
And play their intertwining games
While I edge off to forest dark
And seek so sought-for sleep
In arms of eternal Love.

Take me to the lair of your loveliness—
To the place that is no place—
Where there is song without singing
And love without word.
Take me where I want to be.
Take me into your boundless Being
Where no thought limits.
Take me into my deepest heart
That opens into You.
There at the center of all loveliness
Will I be lovely.
Of all holiness will I be holy.
Of all peace will I be peaceful.
There will I be your begotten.
There will I be we!

The sun seems stolid, unmoving,
Yet its fire fuels the earth.
So, too, Beloved, is your Presence in my
    core—
Still and abiding—
Yet its love fires the whole of me,
A fueling of a finite with infinity.
Let me rest in your fullness—
Projecting nothing,
No thing imaginable,
Just rest in your active stillness—
And know the peace of love.
And let me bring You into my day
And show the world your Presence.

Love, let me settle in the Now.
Too many calls to confusion,
This life we lead.
It drags with a past,
It pulls to a future,
But there is neither past nor future—
Only Now,
Where You are.
And You are the all of my need,
The fullness of my emptiness.
When I sing,
Only of You do I sing.
When I love,
Only You do I love.
For all the songs and other loves
Are in You,
And each note of my song
From a thing of your doing.
Beloved, let me love and sing
This whole Now through.

No frugal fuss with the world's wealth.
Spore and sperm search everywhere for
    change.
Dust dances till stars are born
And no void not filled with form.
Nothing niggardly in God's going.
Prodigal your pace.
The world's anxious to become.
Babies birth by the billions
In an ongoing march to betterment
Out of God's gleeful giving—
Self made manifest in form.
The world is because God is.
Glory, glory, glory to the God who gives!

A round room with no egress—
No ladder to climb, no door to open—
Just a merciless mind of narcissism.
Around and around I go
With no way out,
Only walls of self that keep me in.
I am my own god in my own self.
Only You can make the chamber change
And pull down the circling walls.
And if not, Love, make windows
That I may see your face
And leave the prison of my mind
Or one day build a door
That I walk out from me to You
And all the freedom of infinity.

Choosing life is Center-living.
Barren are the acres of acquirements:
All their produce dies.
The silent Center is where soul sings,
Treasure house of the real's riches,
So empty is forever full.
Everything in the nothingness of Love,
For the empty Center is full of Love
And Love gives all of Self to self.
Beloved, You set before me life and death
I choose the empty fullness of life.

Physics is not knowable.
Magnitude mounts to mystery:
How far the star that's farthest,
How small the speck that's smallest?
Is the universe but an atom
And the speck speckless energy?
What is the realm of the real, Beloved:
Only You, only You.
I do not know the world,
Only You, only You, only You:
You are the only fact.
The world is mystery.

All things pass away:
A coming is a going to be gone,
A flare, a spark, then back to You.
You are Source and End of all.
You speak as You would a word,
And out of the heart of You we come,
Then into the heart of You we go,
Flesh for a while, word forever.
Life of all life, I am in the flesh,
But I am word as well.
Let me speak your Word well
While I am in the flesh,
Before my flesh fails
And I fall back to You.

You who breathe when I breathe,
Whose heartbeat is in the beat of my own,
No cell slides throughout my frame
But You are in it, Beloved,
Bone of my bone, flesh of my flesh.
I am all and ever in You.
My "I am" is a "You are."
First in the real is You:
You are ever in my day,
Giving Yourself to me
That I give myself to You.
And when giving self to other,
You are me and I am You.

You are the beat of every being,
The pulse that pushes time.
Potency becomes act in You.
Each wonder wends its way to surface,
Bounding from your bounty.
The throb of the heart awaits your thrust
And a wing flaps yet again.
How moving your constancy
Toward ever better beings,
Yet they are all as one
In your eternal Now,
Where the moving are still
And the still, moving.
And to think of my own *I am*—
My *I am* is now and yet forever,
Held holy in your You.
My God! Beloved, we are one.

Love, loose my mind from thought:
Concept never capture
Who conceive the all of You.
Loose my tongue from word—
What word speak infinity?
No—thought knows not, word not say
But love knows and love says.
Love reaches to the corners of infinity
And lights upon your loveliness.
Beloved, make empty my mind,
Dumb my tongue,
Wide my heart.
Wound what You will,
Slay what You must.

Silent, still, dark, and empty—
There, there is light and life
And the sound of silent psalmody
And infinite spokes to the unending.
The infinite and the eternal,
All that is, is there,
Not in singularities, but in the all of being.
For You are in my Center
And all being is in You—
All sound in your silence,
All extremities in your endlessness,
Lambent light from your dark Presence—
And all that's dead, living in You.
Beloved, let me be silent,
Let me go deep,
All light denied.
Let me die to all
To live in You.

I must down to the desert,
Where in solitude love lives,
Where bride and groom bring lips of love
And in the stillness make that love
That births another Christ.
I must down to my Center,
Where You wait with tenderness
And I with nothing of the world
Come tryst as your beloved.
Let me leave the world now,
All thoughts and words abandon,
And come to the desert of my Center
Where You form in me the Christ.

Oh the honesty of a *yes*,
The integrity of a *no.*
The world works with *yeses* and *nos*:
It is what it is and never other.
The gull trusts the *yes* of wind
And lays its body thereupon.
The grape trusts the rays of sun
And stores the promise of its wine.
No star circles but is encircled
By the *yes* of yet another.
Then why, Beloved, do my lips say *yes*
When my heart says *no?*
Why do we mean other
Than what is in our heart
And build so tall a tower?
Your *yes* is always *yes*,
And *no*, always *no.*
Never do You deal deceit.
Beloved, put the truth of my heart
Always on my lips.

Beloved, I would You would my window
    wash
That I could then see out.
But You are in my house
As a heart before a hearth,
For mine to join with yours
And feel the flames of love
With hand so easily in hand.
No, it's not the windowpane to blame,
Though You are out of house, as well.
'Tis I not come to sit with You
And feel the warmth of Presence.

Gift, all gift, your giving.
Let me open to receive:
Stretch me to infinity,
That I hold the all of You.
No time pass, so no thing change,
Eternal and infinite in your nothingness,
That in the stillness, all motion,
And in the silence, every sound.
Let no thought despoil,
For how can You be in thought?
Let no word ruin, word is my making.
Only silence, stillness—open to love.
Beloved, make a forced entry if You must
But gift me with your Presence.

Beloved, let me stay in *isness* more,
Where the real everywhere abounds,
For You are in the real, only in the real.
When I get lost in me,
The real and You I lose,
Becoming a water drop
Deep in the middle of the ocean,
Thinking myself the only drop.
Yet when I am in *isness*,
Where the real and You abound,
I flow with all the myriad
In the infinity of your fullness:
The real and You as one.

Soon will come the leaves of grace
That flood the trees with living,
And barren bark and trees will dance
And whisper joy with greenery.
Long, long the winter has been,
Bleak and stark and cold,
Wherein the heart is rendered wry.
But a broken spirit You'll not spurn,
Nor forsake a humble heart.
So soon the leaves of grace will come
Out of the very core of me,
Where You have been this long, long
    winter
Preparing in me a verdant spring.

Tired, tired of the running and the fleeing—
Up mountains of illusion,
Across fields of folly,
Into deserts of delusion—
Fleeing, always fleeing your footfall.
And I carry such false selves with me:
Not one, but legion, are my devils.
Even when I pray,
A self is watching self.
When will I lose all of me
To be in all of You
The whole day through, only You?
Catch me, stop my fleeing,
Slay my devils, free me.
Only in You do I find life.

How happy, when I am not,
When all of me is out of me
And among the wonders of your real.
Let them pull me, Love,
Out of self-containment.
Let each leaf enlist the all of me,
And the colors of a single flower
Cull from me an ecstasy.
Let me never be in myself
Save at Center, where I am not.

How they hide in ambush,
These foes of a thousand faces.
When I war with one,
Another promptly presents,
And so from foe to foe I fight,
In fear I will succumb.
But You are my savior:
No battle lost if You hold shield.
When will I learn to simply walk
With my hand caressed in yours
And forget all fight and thought of war?
For your love slays the foe,
And in that love I live fearlessly.

A duck drops to placid pond
In the dim light of evening hour,
And, gliding without motion,
Is guided to a feeding place.
So my soul lights in You
In the serenity of my Center.
There, without my doing,
I am fed the nectar of your Presence,
Always in the still and quiet.
Beloved, let me drop more frequently
Into the placidity of your Presence.

Beloved, pierce my armor of defense,
The many battlements surrounding soul,
The psyche and all its needs,
Protecting my false-self values.
Thrust a spear straight through
'Til it pierce the heart
And let You as Love pour in
And with, dissolve all protective plates,
Never again weary in their keep.
These only—peace, love, and Presence—be.

How lovely to sleep in your arms,
Knowing tomorrow is your today.
I rest in the peace of your Presence,
Where Love loves eternity-long.
You parent me like a mother,
And like a father you forever protect.
And when I come to You fleshless,
I'll not sleep, but only rest
And know You as You are.

It lies upon the land,
Your loveliness, Beloved.
Like sun it feeds all,
All upon which it falls,
Streaming as shafts of forest light
To the tender shoots below.
Treetops glisten with its kiss
And no crack or crevice denied.
Such is your Love.

The world within the world
Is where I want to go,
Down to the deepest level
Where there is naught,
Not anything—
No stone or star,
Or bug or bud,
No atom, or even quark,
Just the world beneath the world,
The placeless place
Which no one can define.
And I, there, have no eye or arm
Nor psyche that protects the self,
Only a spirit that is free
To love-join with the Spirit,
The Formless One who forms all forms.
O Source, O Love, O Mystery,
When I pet my cat,
Let it be with loving fingers.
For when I pet him,
I pet You.

There is longing in the lingering,
My Source and End so sought.
I am in the flesh now
And flesh has many needs,
But all are satisfied in You.
Flesh longs to be soul-sated.
Fully fleshed or falling away,
It wants only You.
Be with me fully in the flesh,
Be with me when it falls away.

How holy the heart
That abides in its Center:
It delights in your precious Presence,
All it wants, all it ever wanted,
Satisfied in the infinity of Love,
All other loves subsumed.
Lover, lace my other loves with Love.
Draw them as a magnet.
Let them align and be one,
Abiding in my love of Love.

Beloved, not always have I loved You,
Left long in your arms to sleep,
But now with the dawn I awake
And sing as birds my joy
And in all the day's doings
Know your residing love.

O Majestic One,
You weren't in the wind, the quake, or the
    fire,
But in the soft sweet whisperings
That fall away to nothingness
And heard with the ear of the heart.

Like prints in the sand
That stop at the sea,
So let my words stop
And me be lost in the Sea.
There in the depths will I be free,
In the depths of your surrounding love,
Peaceful and secure,
Lost in your love,
Found in your love.
Never more to imprint the sand,
The Sea of Love never leave.
Beloved, I trundle toward the Sea.
I long to leave word-prints behind.

Who writes?
Am I pen or person?
Pen, and You write;
Person, and I write myself.
How I yearn to be but pen
And your words wing the thoughtless
And tumble truthfully on page
With all the limitations of pen, perhaps.
But pen writes the writer only.
A person writes the self.
Beloved, let your love-ink flow
From out my Center
Before it ever touch a page.

There is no time for You.
You live in the eternal Now.
But I live in time,
Save when I live in the Now.
Then I am with You and the real,
Only a presence without time,
No past, no future—just Now.
Would that my Nows were pure
Ever in eternal Now.
That grace You will extend to me.
Little Nows now,
But fully when You call me home.

Beloved, birth in me the Holy One,
The One who lives for You.
Let the Son of your fleshless nothingness,
Filled with the everything of You,
Take flesh in me.
Let all things pall save his presence.
Then will Carmel display its splendor
And the steppes blossom and bloom
And the dry land fill with birdsong.
Beloved, give me heart for emptiness
And be my vacuous fullness,
That Christ be born in me,
And I in Him.

Creator, what make You of this, your
    world?
Look, the lake runs smooth to wood beyond
And trees stretch adoringly to sky
While birds beat home the downing sun:
Too many wonders not to marvel.
And the blending—
A panoply that saves from solitude
By fitting parts into a togetherness that's
    One.
Oh, You are so in evidence this night,
So much numinosity, so many epiphanies.
How clearly You speak to me.

This duality, Beloved, let it be done with.
Oh to live in the Eden of the everyday!
Where all forms are siblings,
And each calls me to play
And be one with them
In a game of goodness gathering.
How lovely not to be, so as to be.
And when You call and come
To walk with me
In your garden of delights,
I will ask kin to halt our play,
So as to listen as You talk to us,
O Lover of us all.

Night noises drift through shadowy trees—
The wind and far-off traffic,
They sing in different tones
The poetry of the real.
But there'd be no music
Did not all things touch
And in this meeting make the music
That sets the trees to dance.
'Tis in the One that music's made
And trees dance steps of God.
You sing and dance all night,
While I rest before the morn.

What say You, that I may say?
Ah, but You do not speak in words—
Only in the silence of love.
I fracture love by words,
And for every word said
There's infinitely more not said.
Your Word is Love,
Your Word is Self, given,
And You are infinite.
Better, then, to sit in silence
And know that You are God.
And to simply let You love me
In thoughtless joining and embrace.
Ah, you're such a lover, Love.
Teach me to give self, too.

To sit quietly in sight of the swan's glide,
To hear the busy business of the birds:
Complaint of crow, thrill of thrush,
Gull groping for the lifting air,
Leaving the water to wake and complain.
And should I spend the day,
I could not tease all out
These sounds and sights of Eden.
To sit purely with quiet mind
And leave an imprisoning self—
This is to live, to go deep, deep into the real
And find You, our common God
Spilling goodness into the finite.

You are where You are—
And You are everywhere.
Beloved, let my Center see You
In the center of all phenomena,
And there know You—
As the singularity in diversity.
You are there, subject in every dwelling,
Being beautiful, being good,
Folding all into your single whole.
Only from my Center,
The seat of my knowing,
Love-bonded with You,
Can I see your Presence
In the commingling community
Of all that is—
The cosmos and all that's in it.
Beloved, draw me ever deeper,
That heart and eye of soul
See You everywhere.

Lo the autumn burns with blaze,
A scorching of the earth's last life,
Rendering a verdant wood on fire,
Death dealt leaf by leaf,
Portent of the stark winter
When wry arms twist in supplication
For yet another spring.
But there is beauty in the burning.
Colors paint a countryside—
While the world waits and submits.
But death so beauteously dealt
Is not death but font.
There is no spring without a fall.
And each burning leaf goes gladly—
As eucharist to font more life.
Beloved, let my body blaze
With the beauty of my autumn,
And when some wind wins it away
And floats it to a ground—
It shall be a eucharist
And I shall be with You.

You draw me, Beloved,
Like a nearby star to black hole.
Whether I am willing or no,
My pen writes your word.
Were I to struggle, it would not avail.
I spin around the vortex of my Center
And fall ever deeper into the unknown,
Where nothing that I know is known
And a stretching of word and thought
Pulls their meaning into nothingness,
Meaninglessly in my Center.
My world is welded new.
Knowing by unknowing,
Pressed into nothingness,
I am one with all.
You at the Center pull all to union,
One with Oneness.
Time and space conflate to stillness.
Brightness and joy compact
In the silent stillness of the Center.
Beloved, suck me in—never to escape!

Lover, let me feel your pulse—
The vigor that courses the world—
See your sunsets, marvel at your birds,
Know the stretch of stars
That fire a frigid world.
Let me hear You in crash of sea
Or in the rhythm of a rain
And taste and smell as at a banquet
Your sumptuous, succulent world.
Beloved, let me let go,
Go out of my world and into yours.
For You are there, everywhere,
And I am only here.
Beloved, come take me by the hand
And lead me out . . . and into!

Look, Beloved, your woodland weeps
With tears of joy,
And, in the passion of a dance,
Mates with an insistent wind.
And You are in it all, Beloved—
The wind, the rain, the dancing leaves.
This is how the many live your Oneness.
You are the One
The many, in many ways, reveal.
Each has your goodness,
Your beauty, your truth.
And since the source is one,
The many are one in their source,
God revealing God.
How holy each thing—being from Being.
Beloved, let the rhythm of the swaying
    trees
Pull me into Now.

Beloved, draw my hand to page.
Push my pen to play
The music of your love.
Let strain after strain intertwine
And leach love from its source
And, singing, sing it on a page.
For the page is for a world
That waits upon the love of Love.
Love lifts and sources singing.
Love is dressed in joy.
When love speaks, joy sings.
So, Beloved, speak a love-word to me
And let me sing—sing it on a page
And carry the word in my heart
And its song all the day long.

Beloved, your wonders are book to me,
A sacred scripture writ—
Every grain a world,
Each mountain a poem.
In this scripture You sing as well—
In forest buzz or call of bird,
In a symphony of exploding skies.
Creatures crawl, fly, run,
Planets orbit, suns dance—
Incessant motion out of stillness.
Mystery piles upon mystery,
But each runs a root to You.
Beloved, You write so exotically
From your book of wonders.
What will You write today?
I can hardly wait to read it!

I ask and ask, and importune:
Send the Spirit.
I yearn for her gifts.
My heart seeks only Her.
You can keep the egg and the fish,
Just send me the Spirit.
For my heart is made for Her,
Nor will it rest except in Her.
Beloved, I ask again, I importune:
Give me the Spirit as you would those
    loaves.

Beloved, let's tryst in silence today.
That's your only language,
And You speak so eloquently.
My language is in words.
But vanities leak into words
And cause cacophony,
And the silent self
No longer speaks its silent truth.
True language is true love
Without the fracturing of word.
Love has no parts,
It is total in self-giving,
Wordless in its silent saying.
Beloved, let me end my words now
And tryst wordlessly with You.

All royalties from the sale of this book
are donated to
Contemplative Outreach and Friends of Silence